Live Your Potential and Let Your Words Lead You to Success

Live Your Potential and Let Your Words Lead You to Success

By JOANN YOUNGBLOOD KING

JYK Publishing
New York

Copyright ©2022 JoAnn Youngblood King

All rights reserved. No part of this book may be used, reproduced, distributed, or transmitted in any form or by any means, graphic, electronic or mechanical, including photocopying, recording, taping or by any information storage retrieval system without the prior written permission of the publisher, except in the case of brief quotations embodied in critical reviews and certain other noncommercial uses permitted by copyright law.

This publication may be ordered at the address below:

JYK Publishing
95-22 63rd Road, Suite 154
Rego Park, NY 11374
www.jykpublishing.com

Because of the dynamic nature of the Internet, any web addresses or links contained in this book may have changed since publication and may no longer be valid. The views expressed in this work are solely those of the author.

The author of this book does not dispense medical advice or prescribe the use of any technique as a form of treatment for physical, emotional, or medical problems without the advice of a physician, either directly or indirectly. The intent of the author is only to offer information of a general nature to help you in your quest for emotional and spiritual well-being.
In the event you use any of the information in this book for yourself, which is your constitutional right, the author and the publisher assume no responsibility for your actions.

ISBN: 9780578287522 (pbk)

ISBN: 9780578287539 (ebk)

Printed in the United States of America

This book is lovingly dedicated to my brothers,
Alvin Youngblood,
Joseph Youngblood III
and the memory of Ronald Youngblood

CONTENTS

Acknowledgements viii
Introduction 1
Chapter 1: How words can haunt you 5
Chapter 2: You can create a new reality with words 11
Chapter 3: How your complaints make your world smaller 17
Chapter 4: Unleash the power of positive words 25
Chapter 5: How words and ideas can change our world 31
Chapter 6: How words guide our modern technology 35
Chapter 7: The case for leaving some words unsaid 41
Chapter 8: How words can change your brain for the better 46
Chapter 9: Words that may be used to manipulate you and others ... 52
Chapter 10: How you can use your words to grow your success 60
Appendix 67
Conclusion 71
Bibliography 72
About the Author 74

ACKNOWLEDGEMENTS

To my family, friends, clients and all the other special people in my life, which are too many to mention, I truly appreciate you.

I would like to thank Electra Ford for her continued support to always hold me accountable and keep me focused on my success.

I would also like to thank my mentors, Daisaku Ikeda, Les Brown, Iyanla Vanzant, Oprah Winfrey and Greg Reid, who are a wonderful source of motivation, guidance and encouragement for me.

My sincere gratitude and appreciation to Maria de Graaf for her invaluable help with this project.

And, lastly, a special thanks to my son, Julian, for simply being my overall motivation. Love you!

INTRODUCTION

The most powerful tools you possess to bring you success in this world are the words that you speak, write and read. As each word is uttered or considered, a corresponding path opens in your mind and in the minds of others.

Your words have the power to change your life and the world of everyone around you. When used wisely, your words are a significant catalyst for change.

What you say can advance your career or sink it, enhance your relationships or demolish them, and nurture your ideas and beliefs or push them into oblivion.

The most significant, life-changing collections of words can be as short as one word or two or as long as a thoughtfully written book. It's all about impact and interpretation.

Guilty. Not guilty. Short words that signal a life of imprisonment or freedom.

Marry me. Let's still be friends. Two short messages that offer a life of love and togetherness or the disintegration of a relationship.

We lost him. He made it. Three little words tell the story of death or survival.

You're hired. You're fired. Two words open up the doors to the career of your dreams or turn your life and source of economic stability upside down.

They won. They lost. They're safe. They're lost. I can't hold on. I can hold on. Come in. Go away. All of these utterances use the same amount of words, but their impact is miles apart.

Words make a tremendous difference in determining your destiny. They can lead you to reach your full potential in life and allow you to engage fully in purposeful work and relationships, or they can take you down a dark road to a disconnection from the world and all its wonders. They can push you to reach your goals or stand resolutely in your pathway, blocking you from reaching your destiny.

You don't have to be a poet or a wordsmith to find the words that change your life and the lives of others.

Sometimes saying just one word makes all the difference to someone. On other occasions, not saying one word changes a life forever.

This is a book that springs passionately from my personal and professional interest in what happens because of how we use words in our life. While some of the stories I will share stem from my own life and the experiences I have witnessed as a Certified Success Coach, others will reflect the latest scientific research on this subject gathered from peer-reviewed academic journals.

In the process, you will learn how to combine this insight about words into a plan for your personal success.

You will learn:

- How the words you heard in your childhood can haunt you throughout your life and hold you back from what you are capable of becoming
- How your brain responds to words and why words have so much power over you

- How negative words can confine you and make your life smaller
- How positive words can create the reality of your success
- How amazingly constructed strings of words have been used historically to change the world
- How words guide our use of modern technology
- Why sometimes it is best to leave words unsaid
- How words can change your brain for the better
- How to recognize words designed to manipulate you
- How you can use your words to grow your success beyond what you can imagine

My work in helping many people over the years find success in their careers has given me a unique window into watching repeatedly how words can be used to change the way people feel about themselves, their world, and their ability to succeed. I have witnessed people who were deeply wounded by the words heard in childhood learn to find new words to describe themselves and their world and rise to amazing levels of success.

Through my own research and experiences, I became increasingly intrigued at the idea of words as a pathway to success. I wanted to share what I learned and the stories of others to a broader audience as I had done earlier with my previous books, *The Next Top Success Story* and *Live Your Potential and Let Your Faith Lead You To Success* in which I focused on helping readers surrender their fear and learn to trust themselves.

Like my previous efforts, it is a participatory book that encourages you to put into practice the knowledge you acquire. After each chapter, you will be invited to think how you can incorporate the ideas into your own life and engage in a couple of short exercises.

If you are a person who likes to read the whole book first and then do the exercises, you will find them all grouped conveniently together in an appendix at the end of the book as well.

Meanwhile, I hope that the words I write will open up a new way for you to consider the impact of words in your life and heighten your skills in using your words to lead you to the success you seek in life.

When you are finished and have had an opportunity to try some of the ideas presented in this book, send me an email and tell me how it worked for you. I am also available for private coaching sessions.

You can reach me at: JoAnn@liveyourpotential.com.

- JoAnn Youngblood King

Chapter 1

HOW WORDS CAN HAUNT YOU

"A broken bone can heal, but a wound a word opens can fester forever." – Jessamyn West

Jennifer (her name is changed to protect her privacy) looked shocked when her manager asked if she would assume an office manager's role within the farming organization she had joined just a year ago.

"You've been amazing since you first started here," he said. "You are super organized, able to keep track of multiple projects and people at once, and we'd be lost without you. We want to promote you to a managerial role and of course, we'll provide additional training so you can continue to grow in your career."

Jennifer found the words to thank him and say that she would be pleased to accept the new role and was happy to take additional training. But inside she was quaking. She couldn't believe she'd been singled out over the 23 others in her office to take the job.

And even as she experienced success, the words she'd often heard her father say to her kept echoing in her mind.

"You're too stupid to amount to anything," he told her repeatedly. "You're dumb as that post in the field. You better hope some guy is desperate enough to marry you, because I can't keep somebody as stupid as you forever."

When Jennifer became my client, she was in a state of conflict that was keeping her awake at night and prompting serious anxiety attacks. On the one hand she was excited to be starting her new career in management; on the other she was absolutely terrified she would self-destruct and be a failure. She worried she didn't have the brains to do the job, even though she had the training, experience and an impressive IQ.

Jennifer was yet another victim haunted by the words she heard in childhood. Like many clients I had coached before her, her opinion of herself was formed not by the reality of who she was and what she was capable of doing, but by the words of others.

It was a reminder to me yet again that words are so much more than just a means of conveying thoughts and ideas and even demands.

Words chisel out our identities in the innocence of our early years. They shape our beliefs, our behavior, and eventually, our responses and actions in life. They determine how we see ourselves and our world, and in many instances, whether or not we will achieve all that we are capable of.

Words are so powerful they can destroy the essence of who we are destined to be. They can stifle a beautiful imagination and crush a child's creativity. Used negatively, they can destroy dreams and desires and shrink our personalities into non-existence.

The problem is that even when we are children and we are being bullied with words and unpleasant names, the power of these words on us is often cavalierly dismissed by those we trust to protect us.

"Sticks and stones will break your bones, but words will never hurt you," the suffering child is told.

The reality is that words break more than your bones; they break your spirit if they are harsh and hurtful. They break your identity when you are faced with a steady onslaught of insults that undermine your essence. They break your dreams, desires and impose limits on what you imagine yourself to be capable of doing.

Conversely, if they are used positively, they can build you up and encourage you to expand your capabilities and confidence. They can start you on the road to success and allow you to persuade others to support your vision and your goals.

For example, a study led by Ming-Te Wang, assistant professor of psychology in education at the University of Pittsburg, shows that parents who use harsh verbal discipline such as shouting, cursing or insulting their children, aggravate their child's problematic behavior, rather than eliminate it.

Even if parents believe they are yelling at their child "out of love" or "for their own good," the damage is still inflicted. In fact, the negative effects of verbal discipline were found to be comparable to the disturbing effects of harsh physical discipline.

The study, published in the journal *Child Development*, concluded that parents who want to modify the behavior of children would be better advised to communicate with them on an equal level, explaining their worries and rationale to the child. The researchers conducted the study in 10 public middle schools in eastern Pennsylvania over a two-year period, working with 967 adolescents and their parents.

Incidentally, the researchers did not go looking for "high risk" families.

As Wang put it: "There was nothing extreme or broken about these homes." Even in supposedly loving homes, it is not uncommon for parents to yell words and insults at their children in an attempt to get them to change their behavior.

The study was supported by the National Institute on Drug Abuse at the National Institutes of Health.

Meanwhile, a report in the April, 2016 issue of the *Harvard Mental Health Letter* also demonstrated that scolding, swearing, insulting, threatening, ridiculing, demeaning and criticizing children can be as harmful as physical abuse, sexual abuse outside the home, or witnessing physical abuse at home.

The report suggests that, when verbal abuse is constant and severe, it creates a risk of post-traumatic stress disorder, a kind of psychological collapse.

Martin Teicher, associate professor of physiatry at McLean Hospital, a Harvard-affiliated psychiatric facility, said exposure to verbal aggression has received little attention in the past, but it is important to understand how words impact our children.

He pointed out a national study found that 63 percent of American parents reported one or more instances of verbal aggression, such as swearing at or insulting their child.

Other researchers have linked harsh words aimed at children with a high risk of them developing into unstable, angry personalities as adults, narcissistic behavior, paranoia and obsessive-compulsive disorders.

Teicher pointed out that verbal abuse may also have more lasting consequences than other forms of abuse because it is often more continuous. Despite that, it has not drawn as much attention from child protective service agencies, doctors and lawyers as other forms of abuse.

Teicher's additional research on this subject shows that exposure to verbal abuse does affect certain areas of the brain that are associated with symptoms of depression, anxiety and dissociation as well as verbal IQ.

In the end it seems, we are all the products of the words we hear and read. If as a child you heard encouraging, loving words, you develop your self-confidence, your identity and your foundation for success in life. If you were subjected to negative words and condemning and humiliating words, you start your adult life off-balance. You may lack self-esteem and be fearful of allowing your identity to be exercised.

As Jennifer mentioned to me in one of our meetings: "I didn't know that the way my father talked to me wasn't the way other dads talked to their daughters. When I confronted him about it as an adult, he said he was just teasing me and trying to make me stronger, but I took his words to heart. It made me feel terrible about myself and I grew up without any self-confidence. I thought I was incapable of doing anything."

Whether you were demeaned by your parents or a caregiver, or bullied by kids in the playground, you may still be carrying those scars. They can hold you back from what you are capable of achieving.

I have discovered that the way to heal is to find new ways to talk to yourself as an adult. Avoiding negative self-talk and increasing positive thoughts and affirmations can change and enhance your self-perceptions. In the process of finding the words that will sustain you, you will discover the impact that your words can have on others.

When you put the power of words behind you in a positive way, you will discover your own ability to influence, lead and ignite others to support your goals and vision. Most importantly, you will find a way to live the authentic, fulfilling life that you deserve.

In this book I will teach you how you can take control over the harsh words you may have been subjected to in the past, and even those insulting, negative words you may use in your self-talk.

Together we will chart a better use of words to help you live fully in the present and achieve your full potential in the future. In the next chapter, we will start to explore how you can use words to create your new reality.

Something to think about:

As with all forms of abuse, the initial step towards recovering from it is to recognize that it happened. Unlike victims of other kinds of abuse, we are delayed in recognizing it happened by the cultural notion that "words will never hurt you."

The positive news is that the harsh words you heard as a child that may still be rolling through your thought stream can be shut off and replaced with affirming messages and words that truly reflect the person you are now and have the power to become in the future.

Something to do:

Answer honestly: Were you verbally bullied as a child or adolescent? What words hurt the most? What negative words directed at you colored how you perceive yourself as an adult?

Make a list of three things that others told you about yourself that hurt and that keep circling in your mind. We will work through these in the upcoming chapters and help you to remove them from the thought-loop that goes through your head when you feel challenged and afraid that you will not be able to accomplish what you want to do.

Conversely, were you one of the lucky people who grew up with encouraging words? Which of those words gives up courage when you are faced with a major challenge? Which of those words do you share with others to connect with their confidence and reinforce it?

Chapter 2

YOU CAN CREATE A NEW REALITY WITH WORDS

"When words are both true and kind, they can change the world." – Jack Kornfield

Why do some words make you feel warm and comfortable and others make you ill at ease? How is it that some words depict reality while others challenge your imagination?

Much has to do with how your brain processes the words you hear and use. When you gain a keener understanding of how your brain recognizes and interprets words in this chapter, you will be better equipped to use this knowledge to fuel your success.

I've seen people agonize for 10 minutes over the perfect note to add to a standard birthday card, for example, because they want to be sure that they have expressed exactly how they feel. Poets can spend hours on one line to ensure that it perfectly represents the imagery they want you to see and feel. But how does anyone know how another will respond to a certain word? Is it them or is it us if they misunderstand what we are trying to tell them?

The answer to all of these questions comes down to understanding how your brain works and how it responds to words as you hear them and read them.

About 15 years ago, a team of British researchers were able to shed light on this in a groundbreaking study where they used the brain scanning technique of functional magnetic resonance imaging (fMRI).

Through this process a team led by Dr. Sophie Scott, an expert in speech neurobiology at the University College London, was able to see how the brain picks out speech from all the other noises, breaks it down, and works out not just the superficial meaning of words but also the intonation and rhythm of speech.

Scott's research revealed that the brain naturally takes speech and divides it into words and melody or intonation. The words are shunted to the brain's left temporal lobe for processing, and the melody is moved to the right side of the brain, the part that is more stimulated by music.

Scientists have been puzzled for a long time at how our brain recognized speech from other sounds and treated it with more attention. This team of scientists discovered that speech is singled out as special by a part of the brain located near the primary auditory cortex. Not only are the words interpreted there, but the correct interpretation is found for words that have multiple meanings.

When the brain is damaged due to injury or a stroke, for example, this separation explains why sometimes the person can pick up the words but not the emotion connected to them, or vice versa.

How does this insight impact your ability to use words to lead you to success?

It allows you to know for sure that your brain uses two distinct parts to interpret the words it hears. You are conscious now that you must always be aware that while your words are vital to communicating your message, your tone and the way you combine your words also helps your intended message to be interpreted correctly.

In the book *Words Can Change Your Brain,* authors Dr. Andrew Newberg and Mark Robert Waldman took our understanding of our brains and how they handle words one step further. They showed through their research that one single word has sufficient power to influence the expression of genes that influence physical and emotional stress.

For example, the positive words of "peace" and "love" alter the expression of genes to the point that areas in your frontal lobes are strengthened and your brain's cognitive functioning is promoted. Conversely, hostile language or even a single negative word can increase the activity in your amygdala, which is the fear center of your brain. In response, the brain releases stress-producing hormones and neurotransmitters, and the brain's clear function is interrupted. When your body hears negative, angry words, it impacts your logic and reasoning brain centers in the frontal lobes.

According to Newberg and Waldman's research, the longer you concentrate on positive words, the more you begin to affect other areas of your brain. Amazingly, functions in the parietal lobe of your brain start to change when you use positive words, and that begins to change your self-perception and your view of the people you interact with.

When your brain fuels your positive view of yourself, it will sway you toward seeing the good in others. In contrast, when you over-use negative words, you grow your own negative self-image and in turn, view others with suspicion and doubt.

The impact of your words on your brain is so profound that over a period of time, the structure of your thalamus can actually change in response to your conscious words, feelings and thoughts. To complete Newberg and Waldman's theory, they believe that the thalamic changes ultimately affect the way in which you perceive reality.

This is so important because when you are full of doubt and believe that your world is dark and it cannot get brighter, you are in turn painting a word picture of your own unfulfilled destiny. But if you use positive words and grow your positive self-image, that also becomes a self-fulfilling prophecy.

Knowing now that your words affect you profoundly and can even change your brain, how do you translate that information into answers to the perennial question of "why do words matter?"

Words are the pathway to your inspiration and permanent change in your life. They let you free yourself of your self-doubt and move confidently forward to the purpose-driven life that will give you true happiness. They turn what you can imagine into reality and allow you to live your life fully, intently, gloriously and successfully.

Words give you the chance to be the best person that you can imagine and to succeed by using your skills and talents to your utmost ability.

I chose to write this book to encourage you to use your words to empower yourself and others because I know personally how important it is to be mindful of the words you use.

I was one of those youngsters, I mentioned in the first chapter, who often heard the dismissal of insults by an adult saying "words can never harm you." I didn't know then what I know now, and that is how far from the truth that statement is.

I have come to realize that my words, thoughts and the actions I have taken or not taken have everything to do with the words I heard growing up. While these words may not have hurt me physically, they were powerful and made a big impact on my life.

My grandmother, who I shared a bedroom with growing up, used to smoke cigarettes. I detested the smell of cigarettes. One day when she was smoking, I told her that the smoke was getting in my face.

She snapped back: "Well, they say that smoke follows ugly people."

If you knew my grandmother, this comeback was no surprise. At that time, I was more upset with the fact that she didn't stop smoking than the words she said to me.

When I was in my senior year of high school, I decided I wanted to go to college. I remember my father saying to me: "You don't have to go to college; you're a girl. You can just get a good job."

The conversation with my father was centered on whether we could afford the college I wanted to go to and stay on campus. However, he uttered those words to me during the conversation and that was all that stuck with me.

I ended up commuting to college; however, I never completed my degree. I often wonder if that conversation subconsciously had something to do with why I didn't finish the program.

It is very interesting that while the comments of my grandmother, father, and many others I heard may not have affected me at the time, but as an adult now, whenever I am faced with some challenge, disagreement or heartbreak, those words come flooding back to my mind.

I grew up in the "children should be seen and not heard" era. I rarely questioned the things that grown-ups said to me. I may not have agreed with what they said, but I wouldn't dare question them. If I ever had the courage to do so, the response was generally "because I said so."

I have done my fair share of participating in negative thinking and it did impact my self-esteem and the way I viewed others. Based on modern research, now I understand why. I learned as an adult that this kind of negative speech pattern was not getting me where I wanted to go in life.

That is how my thinking about words deepened and I started to develop processes that helped myself and my clients to develop positivity and to let my words lead me to success.

I began to pay attention to the words I used and the words that entered my brain. I discovered first hand how powerful words are and that you and I individually have the choice to decide how we will use that power.

For myself, I decided to let the words I hear and the words I speak empower myself and others, and I can show you how to do that. When you can use the power of words to make yourself and your world better, you will find they also put you on a clear pathway to success.

In the next chapter I will show you how your negative thoughts and complaining can close down your life and blur the opportunities that would otherwise be clear to you.

Something to think about:

Pearl Strachan Hurd warned people: "Handle them carefully, for words have more power than atom bombs." Prior to reading this chapter, did you understand that the words you use to speak and to think could actually physically alter your brain?

Knowing what you know now, how are you considering changing your word usage?

Something to do:

Do you have continuing negative thoughts or phrases that roll through your head repeatedly? How do those thoughts make you feel when you stop and dwell on them?

If you suspect that words are leading you to darkness instead of light, start to consider a strategy for change. In the upcoming chapters you will receive lots of ideas and prompts, but start now to consider your position to change.

Chapter 3

HOW YOUR COMPLAINTS MAKE YOUR WORLD SMALLER

"If we understood the power of our thoughts, we would guard them more closely. If we understood the awesome power of our words, we would prefer silence to almost anything negative. In our thoughts and words, we create our own weaknesses and our own strengths. Our limitations and joys begin in our hearts. We can always replace negative with positive." – Betty Eadie

Just over a decade ago, Will Bowen told the story of an amazing movement in his book *A Complaint Free World*.

The vision of the Board of Directors of A Complaint Free World was to share Complaint Free bracelets with 60 million people, or one percent of the world's population.

Bowen and his colleagues believed that if they could positively transform the attitudes of just one percent of the world's people, it would have a ripple effect, raising the consciousness of everyone.

At the time of penning the bestseller, already 10 million people were on board and they already knew who they wanted to present the 60 millionth bracelet to. It would be to Dr. Maya Angelou, former United States Poet Laureate and mentor to Oprah Winfrey.

She was their obvious choice since when they first began their movement, they adopted her quote as their motto: If you don't like something change it. If you can't change it, change your attitude. Don't complain.

They were able ultimately to meet with her at her home in Winston-Salem and make the historic presentation.

The concept behind the movement and the bracelet was quite simple, but highly effective. Supporters put a purple silicone bracelet on their wrist and then switched it from wrist to wrist every time they complained, until they completed 21 consecutive days without complaining, criticizing, or gossiping. In so doing, they formed a new habit.

Bowen, who founded the movement, wrote that by becoming conscious of the words we use and changing them from negative to positive, allows us to change our thoughts and to create their lives by design.

Today the movement has more than 11 million followers and Bowen, a personal example of how words can lead you to success, has written five books and has a booming career as a motivational speaker.

You might be intrigued by this concept, but another part of you wonders why it matters if you complain a lot and allow negative words to dominate your thought patterns and your conversations.

It's fair to ask what is wrong with complaining. Isn't it good for your mental health to be able to blow off a little steam now and then?

You would think so but it is rarely effective in helping you live your potential and find your true success in this world.

Instead, a little complaining leads to more complaining and soon it is an overwhelming habit. The average person complains about 20 times a day, and that includes even those people who think they really don't complain.

Why do we do that? According to Dr. Betty W. Phillips, a psychologist, people complain about things they perceive to be out of their control.

They also complain when they believe they have been treated unfairly. Others complain to get attention or sympathy.

Constant complainers feel that life owes them something and they complain as a way to express their feelings about competition, superiority, and jealously.

Complaining takes many forms, including whining, nagging, nitpicking, worrying and obsessing about the world's problems and expressions of resentment and depression, all contributing to a sour outlook on the world.

When you allow your words to be negative, complaining words, it is as if you are looking at the world through a dark filter. It is a self-perpetuating habit, since the more you complain, the more you look for things to complain about. Even though you don't feel better after you complain, it is an addictive habit and thus very difficult to break.

That is because your brain, which listens and interprets all your words, starts to accept complaining as the norm. The critical views you express prompt your brain to release stress chemicals and this augments your feeling of frustration and irritability. Ultimately you end up damaging the brain's neural circuits that originally protected you from anxiety and depression.

The stress on your brain caused by constant complaining can have a lasting impact. Researchers have discovered that even a week of stress can damage the neurons in your hippocampus, that portion of your brain that is used to solve problems and for cognitive functioning. Repeated, unrelenting stress even impairs the brain's ability to create new neurons.

Over a period of time, this leads to the physical shrinking of the hippocampus, and this causes a decline in such cognitive functions as memory and your ability to come to terms with new situations.

In a 2008 study by Hampel and colleagues, the researchers also discovered that the hippocampus is one of the first regions of the brain to suffer damage in those with Alzheimer's disease.

Dr. Guy Winch, in his book *The Squeaky Wheel*, suggests we complain more today than ever before in our history, but few of our complaints yield the positive change we want. Instead, we fall into a cycle of still more complaints, broadening our scope to tell our negative words to any new audience who will listen.

This destructive cycle doesn't make us stronger. Instead it works to the opposite effect and we start to feel even more victimized, hopeless and unable to achieve what we want.

Studies show that when we purchase a product and we are unhappy with it, 95% of us don't contact the company we bought it from because we expect we won't get the response we want and we don't want to waste the time to do it. Even when we are upset with our loved ones, instead of finding the courage to talk about what concerns us, we call a friend and complain about them.

Believing that our words don't have the power to evoke the actions we want, makes us feel more and more powerless and we start to feel increasingly bad about ourselves. While you can survive a few incidents of this kind of frustration, if it becomes your life pattern it can seriously compound over time to negatively impact your self-esteem and even your overall mental health.

When your self-esteem is lowered through your constant complaining, it is a short step to becoming paralyzed by fear of failure and rejection. You start to lose your ability to make decisions and your attitude impacts your relationships as you become more defensive in an effort to protect yourself.

Your poor self-image also pushes you to act in ways that are not conducive to living your full potential in life and creating the success that would bring you happiness.

This downward spin intensifies because as Nathaniel Branden, author of *The Six Pillars of Self-Esteem,* pointed out, "we tend to feel most comfortable at home, with persons whose self-esteem level resembles our own."

Branden suggests that high self-esteem people tend to be drawn to other high self-esteem people just as low self-esteem people seek out fellow complainers.

But what if you find yourself out of your comfort group? What if you want to be a positive, non-complainer, but you find yourself living or socializing constantly with mega-complainers?

The results are disturbing. Just as we now know that people who do not smoke themselves but who live with smokers can end up with lung cancer from second-hand smoke, second-hand complaining can still harm your overall brain health.

According to research conducted by Professor Robert Sapolsky at Stanford's Medical School, exposure to just 30 minutes a day of complaining and negativity can physically damage your brain. This includes viewing complaining and negativity on television for half an hour a day.

Dr. Andrew Newberg and Mark Waldman, whose work was referenced in the last chapter, took this research into the impact of complaining on our brain a step further. They discovered that if they put you into an fMRI scanner to take a video of the neural changes happening in your brain, and they flashed the word "No" for less than one second, you would see a sudden release of dozens of stress-producing hormones and neurotransmitters.

These chemicals quickly stop the normal functioning of your brain and slow your logic, reason, language processing and communication. In fact, they discovered that just seeing a list of negative words for a few seconds can make an anxious or depressed person feel worse.

The more any of us ruminate on negative things in our lives, the more we can actually damage the key structures that maintain our memory, feelings and emotions. Ultimately you will find your sleep disrupted, your appetite affected, and your ability to experience long-term happiness and success compromised.

If you go to bed at night and lie there for half an hour worrying about your financial or physical health, you will also stimulate the release of these destructive chemicals. This happens at every stage of our life, from childhood to our senior years.

Knowing the serious impact constant complaining and negative thinking has on you is one thing. But trying to stop doing it is quite another. How do you stop your worry and complaining?

A good technique is to start by asking yourself if the situation you are worried about or complaining about is a genuine threat to your personal survival.

I recently became familiar with Byron Katie's technique, The Work, described in her amazing book *Loving What Is: Four Questions That Can Change Your Life*. When confronted with anxiety about a situation, she advises you to answer four questions:

1. Is it true? (Answer yes or no. If no, move to question 3.)
2. Can you absolutely know that it's true? (Yes or no.)
3. How do you react, what happens, when you believe that thought?
4. Who would you be without that thought?

Often when I get to question four, I realize how light I would feel if this thought were erased from my mind or this worry was lifted from my shoulders. I let it go and am restored to positivity.

Another technique is to identify the negative thought that keeps whispering through your brain and flip it by describing the subject with positive words and images. This will quickly ease your anxiety and reduce your unconscious negative thoughts.

Barbara Fredrickson, one of the founders of *Positive Psychology*, discovered that you need to generate at least three positive thoughts and feelings for each expression of negativity. If you express fewer than three, your personal and business relationships will likely fail.

The work of these researchers also makes it clear that if you want your personal and business relationships to flourish and pave your pathway to success, you will need to generate at least five positive messages for each negative one you make. Expressions of negativity include facial frowns as well as words.

Remember that just as negative words and thoughts change your brain, so do positive ones. Good thoughts kick the motivational centers of your brain into action and help you become more resilient when faced with problems.

Happiness researcher Sonja Lyubomirsky, author of *The How of Happiness,* suggests in her work that if you want to live your full potential and let your words lead you to success, you should often engage in positive thinking about yourself, share your happiest events with others, and savor every positive experience in your life.

Something to think about:

To guard against dwelling on the negativity in your life, focus on solutions. If you keep thinking about what went wrong, you will get stuck in a destructive cycle and there will be no room for the solutions to your problem to be heard. Instead, tell yourself that today is the day you will solve this issue and kick your mind into creative mode.

Write down proposed solutions and consider how well they could work.

If no solutions present themselves, tell your mind to keep searching. Then put your problem on hold and go out and do something completely unrelated to the issue you are wrestling with. Listen to music as you go for a walk, garden a little, or engage your mind in a book.

Later, when you consciously return to the issue that is upsetting you, you will find some solutions present themselves.

Something to do:

If you are trying to break the habit of complaining, start a gratitude journal today. List or write about the things that you are thankful for and that bring joy to your life.

If your negativity stems by living with someone who constantly complains or hanging out with friends who gripe about the world at every opportunity, begin to set boundaries. You don't have to mindlessly agree with them but you can use up a lot of energy and time trying to change their minds and still fail. If they persist, do your best to limit the amount of time you spend with them.

Just as you would not invite a smoker into your home to pollute it and expose you to harmful carcinogens, you do not have to make a lot of time in your schedule for a chronic complainer who refuses to explore the positive parts of life.

At the end of the day, understand that as much as you would like everyone in your life to be happy, you cannot make that happen. We are all responsible for our own happiness and well-being.

Chapter 4

UNLEASH THE POWER OF POSITIVE WORDS

"Whatever words we utter should be chosen with care for people will hear them and be influenced by them for good or ill."
– *Gautama Buddha*

I'm always surprised when I start to work with new clients how many of them spend a lot of time telling me how unhappy they are with their current career, which then flows into a litany of what they don't want in the career of their dreams.

"I don't want to work for a person who doesn't respect me," they confide in me. "I don't want to be chained to a desk from 9 to 5. I don't want to have to get permission to create."

The list goes on until I gently interrupt them and ask them to think quietly for a couple of minutes and then tell me what they *do* want.

I need to stop the complaints and negative thought patterns if we are to move forward to helping them secure the successful career they desire.

The first step in living your potential and letting your words lead you to success is to begin expressing yourself in terms of what you want, not what you don't want.

To change your life, you must have the positive viewpoint that it is possible to change for the better and that if you drop your complaints and focus instead on the positive actions that will help you achieve your desires, you will be on the road to making them happen.

From this point forward, if you want to change your life, you have to change your thoughts. Frame your goals with positive words instead of listing what you don't want.

This works because your brain tends to visualize the terms you put into it.

Try this age-old experiment. Close your eyes and think. Whatever you do, don't think of a white bear. Relax all you want but don't think of a white bear.

What do you see when you close your eyes? Likely you see a white bear.

In the timeless psychology book, *White Bears and Other Unwanted Thoughts,* Professor Daniel Wegner reviews the research on why our attempts to control our thoughts often fail. Pulling as an example Tolstoy's short story in which he describes a peer's challenge to stand in a corner and not think of a white bear, Wegner took the white bear experiment to a Harvard University laboratory to test the concept of intentional thought suppression.

Two groups of participants were asked to verbalize their stream of consciousness for five minutes. One group was told they could think about a white bear, and the other was told they could not. In either group, if a white bear entered their thoughts, they were to press a buzzer each time that happened.

While the people told not to think about the white bear pressed the button slightly less than those who had express permission to think about it, at the end of the experiment, they both were close in the times the white bear entered their heads.

Thought suppression, it appeared, was not very effective.

Then the researchers switched the instructions to the groups. Those who had been told not to think of a white bear before were now given permission to do so. Those who earlier had permission were now told to avoid thinking of the white bear.

The results were not the same this time. The people who had been asked to suppress thoughts of the white bear earlier spent much more time talking about it and pressing their buzzers than the other group. The researchers concluded that suppression of a thought leads a person to overindulge in it later.

In practical terms, as we attempt to use words to live our potential, this reminds us that it rarely works to try to control your thoughts by suppressing them. Consider the dieter who tells themselves to not think about having a piece of apple pie. All they can think about is the pie and one day they end up eating half a pie instead of a piece.

When you start to frame your words to influence the changes you want to make in your life, don't do so in terms of what you don't want, because your brain will ultimately seek out just those things. Instead, you must use positive words and word images to depict the life that you do want.

You have to substitute positive words for negative words to develop new habits. You cannot stop thinking about one thought until you have substituted it with another. Your new thought has to be more powerful for you to focus on it and work it into reality.

This means developing your expertise about words that have positive connotations and which paint positive pictures and thoughts. This exercise will be aided by the statistical reality that the English language contains more words that trigger positive responses than negative ones.

We know this because of a groundbreaking study done by a group of researchers led by Chris Danforth and Peter Dodds at the University of Vermont. They discovered that there is a happy bias built into the English language and other languages. Overall, our words tend to be more positive than negative, regardless of whether they are used commonly or rarely.

Their experiment was fascinating. The team of researchers compiled the 5,000 most frequently used words found in four sources. These included 20 years of material from *The New York Times,* 18 months' worth of Twitter, manuscripts from Google Books up to 2008, and music lyrics from 1960 to 2007 for a total of 10,222 words.

Using a service called Mechanical Turk, they then had 50 people evaluate each word on a scale of one to nine, with one being least happy, five neutral, and nine happiest.

At the high end of the scale were positive words like pleasure, comedy and love and negative words like terrorist, rape and cancer. Some words, like "the" or "and" scored truly neutral, getting fives from all the evaluators.

Some words did not fall into a consistent positive or negative category. These words included "pregnant," "beef," and "alcohol," for example. The researchers said that these words assumed the emotion of the context in which they were presented.

In the results of the study published in the academic journal *PLoS ONE,* the researchers eliminated any words with an average score of between four and six because they would not change the overall result.

The happiest word was laughter and the least happy was terrorist.

Some of the happiest words identified included loving, party, work, love, peace, win, gold, parties, successful, song, comedy, celebration, funny, excellent, thanks, enjoyed, victories, pleasure and succeeded. Some of the most negative words were war, funeral, cancer, violence, murder, killing, failure, abuse, jail, injury, terrorist, wounded, unemployment, rape, sad, disaster, cocaine, damages and lawsuits.

Some other words in the top 100 happiest words included happiness, excellent, joy, rainbow, smile, pleasure, healthy, congratulations, weekend, jokes, rich, victory, Christmas, free, friendship, fun, holidays, loved, loving, beach, kissing, sunshine, delicious, outstanding, paradise, sweetest, vacation, butterflies, flower, great, sweetheart, chocolate, heaven, splendid, attraction, hero, hugs, glorious, kisses, promotion, family, gift, humor, romantic, cupcakes, festival, honor, relax, angel, b-day, bonus, brilliant, diamonds, holiday, lucky, mother, super, amazing, profit, finest, champion, kitten, sweet, blessings, bright, entertaining, exited, millionaire, prize, shines, awesome, genius, achievement, cake, cheers, exiting goodness, hug, income, puppy, earnings, interesting, praise, roses, Saturdays, faithful, heavens, cherish, comfort, extraordinary, hilarious, optimistic, peaceful, romance, feast, attractive, glad, grandma, internet, pleasant, profits and smart.

What we learn from these experiments is that words not only prompt negative responses in our brains, but they also are responsible for positive reactions.

While words cannot change reality, they can change how you view your reality and how others view you and your capability. Your words are the filter through which the world interprets you and decides whether to help you, impede you, or ignore you.

When you create your image as positive and use positive words in your transactions, people will be more inclined to want to do business with you, or to hire you. When others describe you as "friendly," or "pleasant" or "dedicated," others are inclined to like you and to help you secure the jobs you want and the promotions you seek.

In the same vein, when they describe you in negative terms as "difficult," or "opinionated" or "depressing," others will be predisposed to see you as a problem even before they say their first "hello" to you.

By now, you are beginning to see how your words and ideas can start to change your world and the world of others. In the next chapter, we will explore that further.

Something to think about:

How would your friends or colleagues describe you to others? Would they use a lot of positive words, or would they sprinkle the description with negative terms as well? Just as importantly, how are you describing yourself?

How do you portray yourself on your social media accounts? What words do you include in your profile? Have you analyzed the words in your résumé? Do you express your capabilities in positive terms? Do you make it clear what you can do as opposed to what you can't do?

Something to do:

Focus on the words that are most commonly used by you in conversation. A good way to do that is to look at an email, record a conversation or take notes while you are someone else talks. Are you sprinkling your daily chats with loads of positive words that people respond to favorably, or do you see the darker, negative side of things and describe your day, your work and your home life through a filter of negativity?

Tomorrow, make a conscious effort to get through the day using only positive words with happy connotations.

Chapter 5

HOW WORDS AND IDEAS CAN CHANGE OUR WORLD

"No matter what anybody tells you, words and ideas can change the world." – John Keating

The premise of this book is that your words can change your life, help you live your potential and lead you to success. Before we delve further into what you can do with words to make a huge difference in your life, it occurred to me that to prove this premise, I needed to show examples of how people have historically used their words and ideas to change all of our worlds.

Prior to the time of Charles Darwin, the world considered that it was obvious that in times of crisis, the biggest and the strongest of us would be the most likely to survive. Then he wrote: "It is not the strongest of the species that survives, nor the most intelligent that survives. It is the one that is the most adaptable to change."

All of a sudden, adaptability, flexibility, and resiliency became sought-after traits, beating out both brawn and brains in qualities most desired for survival.

A whole world of possibility opened up for ordinary people when Leo Tolstoy wrote: "Everyone thinks of changing the world, but no one thinks of changing himself."

Mahatma Gandhi changed our perspective of meekness when he penned the words: "The weak can never forgive. Forgiveness is the attribute of the strong."

Who can ever forget the words uttered by astronaut Neil Armstrong as he stepped for the first time onto the surface of the moon in July, 1969? He said: "That's one small step for man, one giant leap for mankind."

Our world was changed on Aug. 28, 1963 when Martin Luther King delivered his "I Have a Dream" speech during the March on Washington for Jobs and Freedom. To set the scene for his words, keep in mind that he was the 16th out of 18 people speaking that day, so you can imagine that the crowd might be experiencing attention lapses and feel that they had heard enough.

But his words when he stood up and spoke before the 250,000 civil rights supporters from the steps of the Lincoln Memorial in Washington, D.C. are still the defining moment of the American civil rights movement.

His careful choice of words reminded his audience that they could not wait any longer to take action, and his quoting of such well-known documents as the Declaration of Independence added both authority and familiarity to his address.

Addressing Americans in the height of the Great Depression, when people were hungry and jobs were non-existent for many, it would take amazing words to open the darkness with a ray of light.

The vibration of music can touch your heart and soul. The feeling you can get from listening to music coupled with the words of the song, can bring you to a powerful place. There are also times when listening to music, we can get caught up in the rhythmic patterns and the beat, especially when dancing and we may not pay attention to the words of the songs we're dancing to.

When I was a teenager, I loved singing and dancing to all types of songs. I wasn't concerned with the words, I was just having fun. As I got older and realized how much the words I heard and said affected my life, I made a conscious effort to focus on songs with positive messages. Listening to, singing and speaking words help to tap into your potential for success.

I remember listening to Stevie Wonder songs and thinking to myself, "If people just acted on the words of his songs, the world would be in a better place." I loved his songs titled "Loves in Need of Love Today", "I just called to Say I Love You" and "Ebony and Ivory."

Some words we hear, whether in a speech or a song are more memorable than others and stay in our hearts and minds for a very long time. The following quotes stand as testaments of how one person's words can push us forward and establish a new way of being and of seeing the entire world:

"When you arise in the morning, think of what a precious privilege it is to be alive – to breathe, to think, to enjoy, to love." – Marcus Aurelius

"You've got more potential than you could use in a thousand lifetimes; I see world class potential in you. But one of the secrets is you're as good as the best, you don't have to be better than the rest." – Denis Waitley

"Determination and perseverance move the world; thinking that others will do it for you is a sure way to fail." – Marva Collins

"Seize the moments of happiness, love and be loved! That is the only reality in the world, all else is folly." – Leo Tolstoy

"A dream written down with a date becomes a goal. A goal broken down into steps becomes a plan. A plan backed by action makes your dreams come true. In the end, the extent of our own success will be measured by the accomplishments we have helped create in others." – Greg Reid

This is a good time to consider some of your favorite speeches and quotations and try to figure out why they resonate with you. What kind of imagery touched your heart, which words were the most powerful? Did the speaker use repetition of the juxtaposition of words to make them more memorable?

As we move on in this book and you consider first-hand how the power of your words can change your life, understand how they can be used most effectively to express your point of view in a memorable way.

Words continue to change our world, and never is that more evident than with the dawn of new technology that has altered how we live, how we stay in touch with friends and family, and how we work. We will delve into that in the next chapter.

Something to think about:

Think about the last speech that you heard. Was it your graduation speech? A toast at a wedding? An address at a community fund-raiser? A local politician talking about a community policy? Do you remember anything that was said? Was there any quote that you heard that you wanted to save and remember? If you can't think of a single thing about it, is it possible that it just didn't connect with you? Do you still care about the cause or action it was advocating?

Something to do:

Think about one cause that matters to you passionately. Write just one short paragraph of words you would use to persuade someone else to care about it as well.

Chapter 6

HOW WORDS GUIDE OUR MODERN TECHNOLOGY

"Technology and words grow together." – Author unknown

More than at any previous point in our history, words are leading us to the things we want in life. Thanks to new technologies, and primarily Google, we are using words to create our relationships with the world and to zero in on precisely the information we need to accomplish our goals.

Google has taught us the power that comes with being able to organize our world with words and focus on how they can get us what we want. Whether we are seeking documents, videos, music, images, or maps, we find them by using precise and accurate word search choices.

But Google was not the first piece of technology that impacted how we use words to live our potential and drive us to our success. The invention of the printing press in the 15th century was a revolutionary technology that brought the power of the written word into the hands of ordinary people. New forms of punctuation had to be developed to make words easier to read, and the whole concept of English grammar came into being.

Other new technology like the telegraph, the radio and the television preceded the Internet as impactful developments on our word use and the creation of new styles of speech.

Word choices drove responses during wartimes, and today's political pundits and marketers still spend hours and millions of dollars to find the right, persuasive words that will push people to take certain actions.

But as amazing as this early technology appeared in its day, nothing has advanced the power of words faster and more globally like the advent of the Internet. "Google," a company name became a verb as in "I googled it and…" in the same way that the Hoover vacuum cleaner of a previous generation became synonymous for cleaning the house as in "I hoovered the living room carpet…."

Through emails, text messages and social media postings, we started to develop language to make our points even more efficiently than the dictionaries that were once our word bibles. We now use acronyms like "YOLO" as if they were actual words and indeed, some acronyms have made their way into respected dictionaries.

Spellcheckers were added to our computers to ensure that we spelled our words correctly. Programs like Google Translate and Babblefish help us discern the meanings of words from other languages.

Technology also gave new meaning to existing words and created new ones. Certainly, our ancestors never considered the "storage capacity" of a "Cloud" nor imagined a world where "traffic" had any other meaning than people passing by. Words like "pin," "post," and "tag" had entirely different connotations in the days prior to Facebook, LinkedIn, Instagram and Pinterest.

More recently, the rapid and rising influence of social media sites have helped to evolve our word choices and language, and even introduce symbols (emojiis) to help us express our true feelings.

In terms of word changes, consider how fast the changes continue compared to earlier technological changes that took decades to have an impact. It has only been 20 years since the American Dialect Society selected "google" to become the word of the decade.

When the printing press was invented, educators rejoiced because people finally had access to more information. But the process wasn't instant. The person seeking the meaning of something or the explanation of a theory had to transport themselves physically to a library, find the book, and then read it. It could take days, even weeks to find the information a person was seeking.

Today we have instant access to a global database of amazing facts, ideas, science, philosophy, art and geography at our fingertips. We are vexed if we can't determine what we want to know within two minutes or less. If it takes us more than 20 seconds to understand something, we click on something else assuming that it will be explained more clearly in another location.

This instant access to the knowledge we seek has significantly impacted our society in general and ourselves in particular in terms of what is possible for us to achieve.

We can solve problems faster, advance our ideas farther, and satisfy our curiosity fully. The Internet, seen in its most positive light, is a vehicle that can unify us and the world around us by allowing for easy dialogue. It can drive our success by allowing us to have our words reach a broader, more defined and identifiable audience, and to garner support for what we are trying to achieve.

The Internet, and all that it entails, lets us share our words and tell our daily stories to a broader audience than ever before. In this process, we discover that our words not only mean something to us, but they are also a means to something, and that is our success.

More than that, words empower us as individuals. We can find step-by-step directions to any place we want to go and virtually anything we want to build. We can shop and compare prices and find what we want within the confines of our budget. We can tap into health information, conduct our banking, and access public information. We can access personal connections and build whole communities of people interested in our ideas.

Our Internet connection also allows us to study and take whole university programs on our own schedules without having to physically be present at the brick and mortar. It lets us start our businesses without expensive storefront properties and high overheads.

It is a tremendously positive force for change in the 21st century and encourages us to access and exchange ideas and develop ourselves by gaining great knowledge and insight.

To use words on the Internet to live your full potential and develop your success, you need to learn how to select the keywords that will maximize your searches. If you are creating content, they will also be crucial in allowing other people to find you.

It is this part of the Internet, the honing in on the properties of keywords, that exposes us to the tremendous power of words. We begin to understand how certain words trigger unique responses, and how to use the power of words to infiltrate the minds of people we hope will support our ideas or businesses.

According to the Content Marketing Institute, there are hundreds of trigger keywords that have been found in different scientific studies to activate hypnotic reflexes in your readers' brains.

For example, research by the University of Pennsylvania shows that making yourself and others happy is possible by spreading the word. Related research indicates that people tend to share their happy daily experiences 70% of the time. At the University of California, researchers discovered that not only is happiness contagious, but online communities can actually magnify the intensity of global emotional simultaneous action. In other words, you can spread happiness online and make it even more intense.

Words that are the most delightful of all the happy words that people respond to include: Overjoyed, blithe, gleeful, spectacular, triumph, stunning, breathtaking, miracle, wonderful, victory, excited, sensational, amazing, blissful, uplifting, valor, eye-opening, daring, jubilant, devoted, magic, fulfilling, mind-blowing and heartfelt.

There are so many ways to use your words with power over the Internet. For example, did you know that when you start a post with the word "imagine" that your reader starts to actually imagine?

If you want people to respond directly, use the word "you." The word triggers action in your brain's cuneus, superior and middle temporal cortex and middle frontal cortex. They all spring to alertness when they are directly addressed through the word "you," according to a study by Dennis P. Carmody and Michael Lewis published in the journal *Brain Res*.

Something to think about:

How much thought do you put into the words you use to search and find the information you seek on the Internet? Can you recognize the words others might be using to charm and attract you to their product or cause? Words that are the alphabetic equivalent of a loving mother's hug include: No strings attached, Try before you buy, Cancel anytime, No questions asked, No risk, No obligation, Promise, Support, Certainty, Insurance, Dependability, Reliability, Transparency, Durability, and Trustworthiness, among others.

Something to do:

Never underestimate the power of one small well-expressed sentiment. Think about the many websites that generate high traffic just by offering a collection of quotations.

Think about how these three quotes make you feel and try to pick up the keywords that trigger your emotional responses:

"The only person you are destined to become is the person you decide to be." – Ralph Waldo Emerson

"Happiness is when what you think, what you say, and what you do are in harmony" – Mahatma Gandhi

"Every great dream begins with a dreamer. Always remember, you have within you the strength, the patience, and the passion to reach for the stars to change the world." – Harriet Tubman

Chapter 7

THE CASE FOR LEAVING SOME WORDS UNSAID

"Words empty as the wind are best left unsaid." – Homer

For all the words you say that have value, you will find at some point in your life that the words left unsaid are even more important on the road to success.

We tend to think that those are associated with moments of anger or the disengagement of relationships, but sometimes words you regret spring out of the best of intentions. You give advice to someone who doesn't want it; you try to empathize with someone in distress by comparing some similar event in your life when all they want you to say is "I am so sorry," and leave it at that.

Finding the right words is often a challenge, and just as challenging as knowing when to stop talking and listen.

I can't say I have figured out all the rights and wrongs of leaving words unsaid, but I have learned a great deal about some of them through my years of success coaching.

A big no-no, for example, is to believe that just because you learned something the hard way, others would want you to save them the pain of going through a similar experience. Sometimes they do and they will file away the advice or insight to consider it. But often they prefer to learn from their own experience and as frustrating as that can be when you want to help them or save them from themselves, you have to let them do so.

You will know you are in the danger zone when you justify your interfering words to yourself by your belief that the person is simply not aware of the results of their actions. What one person feels is an acknowledged outcome of a particular action can be the exact opposite of how another person perceives this.

I learned this very early on in my studies when I was trying to apply what I was learning to a family member. That person was up to their eyeballs in student debt and a credit card burden from a bad relationship. They thought that the best way out was to start the business they always wanted. I thought, mistakenly as it turns out, that common sense would dictate that they got a steady job first, paid off some of the debt to make it manageable, and then went into business.

They pretty much told me what I could do with my opinion and pressed on. I am delighted to say, that they achieved success against all barriers. They had a good idea and execution of it at precisely the right time, they worked hard, and they succeeded. They even had the graciousness not to come back to me and say, "see, I told you so!"

I've learned that you must be clear when you give people advice and counsel them that your good intention and your knowledge of likely behaviors is obvious to them. If they are not totally convinced that you have their best interests at heart, it is best to hold onto those words until they ask you: "What would you do in this same situation?"

Another time to leave words unsaid is when your temper flares, when your emotions are running high, when you are experiencing intoxication in any form, and when you are fatigued or wake up in the middle of the night and decide to share what you are thinking.

Social media postings done under such circumstances can come back to haunt you, your career and important relationships for the rest of your life. Once you speak or write certain words, it is like swinging a baseball bat at a wasp's nest. They will get out, they will buzz around, they will attack you back, and you can never get them all back inside on your terms.

There are some word combinations that I would just ban if I could, because when said negatively, I have never seen them elicit the response that the speaker desires.

Some phrases that are best left unsaid are:

"I hate you!"

"You are so stupid!"

"You never listen to me!"

If you find yourself locked into a conversation where your inner voice is pushing for those words to come out, change the topic or don't say anything at all.

Always remember that communicating is a conscious choice. You make the ultimate decision of whether or not you will engage in an exchange of words. How much you disclose or how little is entirely at your whim and within your comfort zone.

You may be burdened by carrying stories you don't wish to share, you may also be carrying thoughts and stories you feel that you must share. If you don't, you believe it will be impossible to move forward.

Sadly, times like these often occur when you are angry, disappointed or otherwise emotionally upset. As hard as it may be during those moments, take time to ask yourself if you can see an identifiable advantage to telling the story. If your reason is that you think you'd feel better if you just got it off your chest, take a few seconds to consider whether or not your theory will work. What if telling that story does not make you feel better? What if it just makes you feel even worse? Are you prepared to risk that?

If a person is opening up to you or explaining an important part of their behavior, and you want to jump in with your story, if you are not sure it will advance the conversation and make it better, just listen quietly for a little longer. We all have a tendency to rush right in to fill the silence as soon as one person stops talking, but when there are just the two of you present, that may not be the best strategy. Sometimes you just need to take a few minutes to digest what is said and if you still seek clarification, a silence that follows a person speaking often prompts them to continue speaking. From those extra words, the nuggets of truth often emerge.

Remember that there is a huge difference between using silence as a gentle probe to keep a person talking, or using silence as a punishment technique to solidify that you don't want to speak with a person. If you want to use silence as a weapon not a tool, you are sending a clear message that you do not want to continue to try to solve the differing points of view with dialogue. What you really want is for the other person to give in to your point of view.

On the other hand, silence is good when we are so angry that we know the words we utter will be regretted later.

How can you tell when leaving words unspoken is a positive act and when it is a hurtful one? You will know instantly if you consider your motive. If you refrain from speaking to illustrate your respect for someone, it is a good motive; if it is to hurt or injure someone, it is a bad motive.

Something to think about:

How often do you consider the motives behind the words that you use? Were you aware that you may be unconsciously selecting words that hurt or words that heal? When you fall silent in a conversation or a heated exchange, are you doing so to avoid saying words you will regret or because you want the person you are arguing with to take your point of view? After reading this chapter, are there words that you will avoid using entirely?

Something to do:

The power of words exists whether you want to use them for good or bad. Think about the last serious verbal disagreement you had with a colleague or loved one. What kind of tactics did you use to get your point of view across? Knowing what you know now, how would you change your verbal exchanges?

Chapter 8

HOW WORDS CAN CHANGE YOUR BRAIN FOR THE BETTER

"Choose your words wisely, because they will influence your happiness, your relationships, and your personal wealth."
– *Andrew B. Newberg*

Words have tremendous power over your mental and physical health, and govern how you think and feel about yourself. You can use your words to work your way back to a happier state of mind, you can use them to ease your anxiety, and you can even use them to secure the job of your dreams.

This reality came to light through the groundbreaking work of psychology professor Dr. James Pennebaker that came to prominence in 1986. He discovered an amazing thing about words when he asked a group of students to spend 15 minutes writing about the biggest trauma they had experienced in their lives. If they had not experienced an actual trauma, he asked them simply to write about their most difficult time in life.

They could let go and share their deepest thoughts. For four days in a row, they were asked to do the same thing. About one in 20 ended up crying, and they were given a chance to opt out, but they always stayed.

Another group was simultaneously asked to just write about something neutral every day.

Then Pennebaker waited for six months to pass, even though he continued to monitor how often the students visited the health center. He was totally shocked with the results.

The students who had written about their dark, secret feelings made significantly less trips to the doctor in the following months.

His discovery opened up a whole new vein of research and in a number of follow-up studies, the clear link between mental and physical health and expressive writing was solidified and proven repeatedly. Being able to pour your words out in a written exercise left people feeling better despite having serious health problems such as asthma, arthritis, breast cancer and migraines. Even wounds healed faster when the participants wrote. That is not to suggest that it cured those health issues, only that those who had them seemed to experience reduced symptoms and made less trips to the doctor.

Next, Pennebaker set out to discover what was impacting his participants: Was it the act of writing of the words people used to express themselves? With his subjects' permission, he was able to look and analyze the kind of words people used as they wrote.

He discovered three things:

1. The kind of words people used changed over the course of the four days. Those whose wounds healed fastest, for example, used the word "I" the most the first day, and then moved to saying "he" and "she" more. Pennebaker interpreted that they were starting to look at the event that impacted them from other perspectives. They also started to use the word "because" more often, which he viewed as a sign that they were starting to make sense of the horrible trauma that had happened to them.

2. The way the participants felt over the four days also altered substantially. On day one, most of the people said the writing

about something painful made them feel worse, not better. Then they started to feel better. Their immune systems were stronger as the exercise continued, even though it did not stay that way forever. As one researcher described it, it was short but powerful.

3. Overall, the people who had major upheavals in their life and who kept them secret were more likely to have health problems than those who talked about their problems. Finding the words to tell their story and writing them down forces the person to organize the event in their mind and to start putting all the pieces together.

Pennebaker concluded that when people write about their emotional upheavals, their physical health actually improves. More specifically, the people who changed their pronoun use from "I" to "he" or "she" as the exercise continued improved more than those who did not.

This led this remarkable researcher to start exploring the link between health and the other things we write: everything from emails to websites to blog posts to the collected works of poets and novelists and playwrights. In his book, *The Secret Life of Pronouns,* Pennebaker described his findings.

He discovered that the person with the higher status uses I-words less. He also noticed that men and women used language differently because they negotiate their way through their worlds differently. Women tend to talk more about other human beings, he discovered, while men talked more about concrete objects and things.

Pennebaker, who has written more than 300 scientific articles and 10 books about word use and its impact on our health, also discovered that as we age, we tend to use more positive emotional words and refer to ourselves less.

In 2015, another team of researchers also delved into what our word choices say about us. Lead author Allison Tackman of University of Arizona and her research team joined up with psychologist Matthias Mehl, director of the University of Arizona Naturalistic Observation of Social Interaction Laboratory to study the spoken and written use of "I-talk" (use of pronouns I, me and my) of 4,700 people from six different labs in the United States and Germany. They found a link between people who used I-talk a lot and symptoms of depression.

At this point, you may be wondering how many references to yourself are normal in the course of a day, and how many border on self-obsession.

Statistically, the average person speaks and writes about 16,000 words a day. Again, on average, about 1,400 of those words (or about nine percent) tend to be first person singular pronouns (like the word I). Mehl's observation was that people who fall into the category of more frequently using I-talk use "I," "me" or "my" up to 2,000 times a day.

How can you reduce your own use of I-talk?

One way is simply to become aware of how many times you are using the word "I" or "me" in your spoken or written conversation. Once you become aware, it is easier to catch yourself from using them as often. You can even ask for help from your friends or a family member to note how often they hear these words from you.

When you are able to reduce your I-talk, the researchers believe that your proneness to negative emotions will be reduced. You could conduct your own experiment over a couple of weeks and determine which week you feel better: the week with the reduced I-talk or the regular week.

But at the end of the day, how do all these things help you live your potential and lead you to success?

The words you use play a major role not only in determining what others think about you, but how you perceive yourself. When you become increasingly aware of this, not only can you enhance your positivity, but you can select your words carefully to give your best impression in job interviews, presentations and debates.

How you describe yourself in a job interview can make all the difference between you getting the job of your dreams or finding yourself stuck in a place you don't want to be just to afford to pay your bills.

For example, it is okay to use I-talk in a job interview, but it is especially important to bring in other circumstances and explanations.

Let's say you are advised that the company needs adaptable people.

You can answer: "I am very flexible about whatever happens."

You've given them I-talk and nothing else.

But if you say: "I am very flexible and adapt easily to unexpected challenges. When I led a team charged with ensuring all our Christmas boxes filled with perishable items were delivered by Dec. 23 and a major snowstorm hit, I handled this by calling in a snowmobiling club and ensuring every last box was where it needed to be by end of day."

Then you have talked about yourself, but you have added perspective and context, and the message carries a punch that just your bland assurance of your flexibility does not.

Carry that example further by ensuring that the words you use to describe yourself carry the exact connotation you want to portray.

If you are detail-oriented and careful to ensure the medicines you handle are properly labelled and stored in the pharmacy, say that instead of describing yourself as "obsessive" which can have quite a different connotation to the listener. "Obsessive" doesn't send the message "I work to ensure all safe-handling protocols are followed." Instead it can mean "I agonize over every pill placement and am annoying to work with."

When asked for your best quality, do you reply that you are "likeable?"

The fact is that if you are likeable, the interviewer has already warmed to your charm; you don't have to tell them. As soon as you do, they stop believing it.

Something to think about:

Have you experienced a severe emotional upheaval or trauma in your life that remains unresolved? Do you have the courage and time to dedicate writing about it for 15 minutes a night and see how you feel at the end of the exercise?

I remember reading about a woman who tried this at one point of turmoil in her life, and even though she was extremely skeptical in the beginning, by the end she was absolutely amazed at how her perspective changed. The thing that kept her a prisoner in her memory turned into the defining incident that brought her, her sense of freedom in the present.

Something to do:

Write three adjectives that best describe your career potential. Next, put them in context by giving an illustration example that illustrates why that adjective is an accurate way to describe yourself.

Chapter 9

WORDS THAT MAY BE USED TO MANIPULATE YOU AND OTHERS

"Leadership is positive influence, not malicious manipulation."
– Dan Rockwell

Kenneth is a client of mine who was concerned that he couldn't find the strength to tell his boss that he felt overlooked in his position and wanted a fair shake at promotions and advanced training.

However, each time he summoned the courage to bring up the topic, his boss dismissed his concerns with assurances that "I'm looking out for you," and "I'll know when the time is right to move you along," or "I'm protecting you; it wouldn't be any advantage to you to set you up for failure, would it?"

Kenneth (whose name is changed to protect his privacy) started to feel totally manipulated, but he didn't know why. He knew his boss appreciated his work, because she repeatedly told him she'd be lost without him and what a great job he was doing. Yet that never translated to sending him to take a course, attend a conference to share his ideas with others, or even to attend higher-level meetings in the company.

When he consulted me, he didn't know if she was right that he just wasn't ready to move up the ladder, or if he should just leave the job, even though he did feel appreciated.

It took a good discussion of the terms his boss used in the conversation with him for me to help him understand how completely he was being manipulated. Clearly, he was a great help to his boss…so big a help, in fact, that she did not want him promoted because selfishly, it would make her job harder.

Kenneth was certainly not the first client I had worked with to fall victim to word manipulation. Prior to our talks, he felt that he would be able to recognize manipulative words, but once he realized how cleverly they could be hidden in compliments, he began to understand what was happening in his life. Ultimately, he had to take action to change it, which in his case involved leaving his job and finding a more fulfilling one where he was allowed to grow and learn.

Anyone who thinks words are just straight-forward collections of letters of the alphabet that mean one thing is someone completely unaware of the power of words and phrases. That power can be used for good, as we observed from the great speeches of some of the world's most respected leaders. But word power can also be used to manipulate people, to enslave them, to hold them back, and to serve the purposes of others.

Most of us are aware that advertisers may use words or phrases to manipulate us (as in a salad dressing that promises to be "95 percent fat free" instead of "contains 5% fat").

We also realize that politicians can be clever about manipulating their followers by making broad promises at election time and gradually reducing them to virtual nothingness once they have secured the vote.

But people with their own self-interest at stake will also use words to manipulate you, and a huge part of living your full potential and using your own words to achieve success is recognizing the signs and word choices that indicate you are being manipulated by others.

In a groundbreaking research project on this subject to illustrate how significantly we react to certain words, Stanford University Psychologists Paul Thibodeau and Lera Boroditsky conducted a creative experiment to see how people interpreted and responded to certain words.

They did a presentation to participants on crime statistics, embedding throughout their test words that described crime as a beast (as in "preying on a town," "lurking in your neighborhood") or as a virus ("infecting your town" or "plaguing the neighborhood.")

Then they asked the study participants what should be done about the crime problem.

Those who were given the statistics that portrayed crime as a beast were apt to propose law enforcement actions such as "capture the criminals," "enforce the law" and "punish the wrong-doers."

But those who received the crime report in which crime was depicted as a virus framed their solution in medical terms of diagnosing, treating and inoculating crime.

This is fascinating because the reality of crime is that it is neither a beast nor a disease. But while people apparently understood that, they nonetheless processed the information they were given in terms of the metaphors used in the presentation. The study reminds us that we are all subject to the manipulation of words.

Even words that are very similar to each other strike different connotations to the ears and brain of the listener. For example, many countries welcome "migrant" workers who are seen as people who move around to find work and often do the jobs that locals don't want to do such as harvesting produce and then leave. However, they fear an influx of "immigrant" workers because they are perceived as people who are coming to live permanently in the community.

We sometimes say communities hard-hit by disaster or tragedy are given "hand-outs" by the government or they are given "aid" or even "emergency assistance." People respond favorably to the concept of emergency assistance or even aid, but hand-outs are viewed negatively.

People who write for a living, such as journalists or influential bloggers, are well aware of the different connotations of words and select them deliberately to create the response that they want. In many cases, there is no deep, underlying mission to make you think one way or the other, but they do want to pique your interest and keep you reading, so they may inject words like "shocking," "terror" or "confidential memo" as a means of moving you to read their story. Others may deliberately be trying to influence your response and will take advantage of words that make the public feel safe and happy and words that encourage unease. So, a person standing up for a cause they believe in is a maverick or innovator, but a person representing a point-of-view they disagree with is a rebel or activist.

It is important as you work to let your words lead you to success that you learn to read critically, consider the source, and weigh the word choices of the person demanding your attention. One person's unruly crowd is another's wildly enthusiastic gathering.

Analyze the information you absorb by studying the verbs used, the tone (whether it is formal or conversational), the time of the report and the place, the emotion conveyed in the report, the potential bias of the source, whether or not different points of view are presented, the purpose of the release of this information at this time, and the point of view (I, we or you). Or is it written in the third person (he, she, it or they) which distances the author and the reader?

Many people skip over titles and introductory paragraphs to get to the gist of the article, but these initial attention-getting words often carry the clues to what the writer is really trying to tell you. In interpreting the words you are reading, it is even important to consider whose words they are. An entrepreneur, for example, may see the world differently and paint a picture that varies from an artist. It does not mean one is wrong and the other is right; it just means that your understanding is enhanced by having an indication of what the person stands for in life.

People like Kenneth, mentioned earlier often have an uneasy feeling they are being manipulated or they are not getting the full story, but they aren't necessarily trained to recognize the phrases that indicate they may be hearing manipulative messages. Much of what passes as apparently harmless teasing or as "good advice" is not designed with your best interests in mind at all. The person teasing or advising is more likely manipulating you to serve their own interest.

How do you recognize these phrases? It can be particularly difficult for adults who grew up being manipulated by parents or care-givers to recognize the signs as adults, because they have become conditioned to respond the way the speaker wishes.

If your mother got you to constantly alter your plans to do what she wanted by using the words "After all I've done for you," for example, you may go through life susceptible to those who play on your guilt to manipulate you. If your father always told you that "everyone thinks you're too weak to make the team," you grow up thinking everyone must be saying that behind your back so they are likely right. You may not realize that is a common manipulative approach to keep you from doing what you want.

Most children are manipulated to perform required behavior with bribes. A parent says "eat all your vegetables and you can have some ice cream for dessert." Or "clean your room and we can go to the movies this afternoon."

Shaming you, threatening you, frightening you and filling you with self-doubt by using words and phrases all signify classic manipulation techniques. The dire warnings of: "You're too stupid to do that," or "who could possibly love you other than me?" or "I can't make it if you leave me," are other manipulative phrases.

Here are some other words and phrases that should be red flags to consider that you are being manipulated:

"I understand your point of view but I have to think about what is best for us and our family."

"Look what you made me do!"

"If you leave, I will kill myself."

"Don't be so dramatic!"

"This is for your own good."

"I am just trying to protect you."

"You're overthinking this."

If you read between the lines in all of these cases, you can see that what the speaker is really saying is "I am in control of you." Nobody has that right to control you. Nobody can make your important life decisions for you. One person cannot force or make another person do something. People who threaten to harm themselves because of what you do, may need professional help and you cannot be a prisoner of their manipulation because it could only get worse for you.

I am not advocating for a minute that when you recognize manipulative phrases that you have to call people out on them. Rather, I am suggesting that you need to be aware that you are being manipulated and make a conscious choice of whether you will allow it to happen or whether you will distance yourself from the person who wants to limit your potential and control your destiny.

If you grow into adulthood carrying the burden of self-doubt and self-blame from childhood verbal abuse or manipulation, it will be difficult to break free, and you may continue to be manipulated by words without even being conscious of them.

If someone humiliates or hurts you and then dismisses your pain as if it is for your own good, it isn't. You can grow up and live strong without having to survive pain and humiliation. Sometimes you hear people remark how they got beaten or humiliated as a child but they turned out okay or got very strong because of it, as if one is the result of another. It is only through therapy that someday they discover they are strong not because of being manipulated or abused, but despite it.

Adults do not have to tolerate being yelled at, threatened, intimidated or manipulated. If you hear words that indicate that is happening daily and you protest, the response is often "don't play the victim." You are a victim, and you have to make it stop. You do not deserve to go through life this way.

It is okay if you refuse to accept the description of yourself other people give. You do not have to feel guilty and ashamed of being you.

Even in the workplace, you do not have to endure toxic and abusive behavior.

As a child dependent for shelter and food on their parents or caregiver, you may have felt you had to tolerate manipulative words. But as an adult, you do not. You can politely assert that the description offered does not really fit you and set healthy boundaries on what kind of behavior is permissible.

(If you find your mental or physical well-being is endangered by other's manipulation, you need to seek professional assistance.)

Something to think about:

Do you have friendships or relationships that leave you feeling manipulated? Do you recognize the words that indicate the other person is taking advantage of you and trying to get you to do what they want? How important are these relationships in your life? Can you change them? Can you leave them?

Something to do:

If you spend time with a person who makes you feel uncomfortable and unfulfilled, listen to their words and try to determine if that feeling is coming from being manipulated.

What words or phrases are being used that cause your red flags to go up? How can you change this relationship by asserting yourself and refusing to be manipulated?

Chapter 10

HOW YOU CAN USE YOUR WORDS TO GROW YOUR SUCCESS

"Without continual growth and progress, such words as improvement, achievement, and success have no meaning."
– Benjamin Franklin

Words have never been more important. With a few well-chosen words on your LinkedIn profile, you can attract recruiters offering you the career of your dreams. With a smattering of poorly-considered words on Facebook, you can bring that dream job crashing down around your ears.

You can use words to fulfill your dreams, unleash your full potential, and to accomplish the success that you seek. The words of others can teach you new skills and expand your thinking. Your words can inspire others to reach new heights and to go after their own dreams.

The power of words is tremendous. If you go through life using positive words, you will see the world as a happier place and transform the lives of those whose lives entwine with yours. If you go through life thinking negative thoughts you can become filled with hate and spew poison that disgusts others or brings them down with you.

One key theme of this book has been a constant reminder that the words you use in your thoughts and in your conversation really do dramatically influence your life and the lives of others. You learn that you don't have to be a mere word receptacle, being filled up with the words of others who may be trying to manipulate you or influence you. Instead, you can use your words powerfully to be your authentic self and live up to your full potential.

Your words have the power to encourage you through your self-talk and support others in your conversations. They can elevate your thinking and allow you to see a clear road to success and follow it with hope and promise as your guideposts. You can weigh the messages of others, consider the source and bias of what you are hearing, and decide for yourself what information is useful and what should be ignored or challenged. That is the most powerful way you can handle the words in your life.

Your words are the energy that fuels your dreams and ignite reactions in others. Every word you utter or write is like a stone falling in a still pool of water. It hits and while you think it has fallen into oblivion, you are shocked to see how far the ripples swirl out from it and how wide a spectrum it can cover.

Generally speaking, the kind and tone of the words you use are the kind and tone of the words that will boomerang back to you. If you speak of ideals and uplifting innovation and hope, you attract people who see your value and work to help you reach your ideas, fulfill your innovative plans and reach your success. If you constantly complain and spew out negative thoughts, you will surround yourself with more negativity, leading to emptiness rather than fulfillment.

Your words are your most important tools in life to lead you to success. Successful people understand this and take firm control over the words they allow through their minds and which they express to others. They are aware that words build your destiny or destroy it, if not used correctly.

How can you use what you have learned in this book to ensure that your words keep you on the path to your full potential?

Here are five ways to change the way you use words in your life and ensure that your words lead you to success:

1) Build a list of word affirmations that guide your thoughts.

Visualize what success looks like to you, and write affirmations that reflect the steps you believe will take you to the success you want and deserve. It doesn't have to be a long list, just a fervent one. In fact, when I decided to change my life and become a certified coach, just before every meal as well as first thing in the morning and last thing at night, I repeated these affirmations:

I will find a way to reach out and help people achieve their full potential in life.

I will be part of a powerful force to make the world a better place.

I will accomplish the certification and training I need to do the job I desire.

I will treat my clients with respect and help them to reach their goal.

I will be a positive force for change in my own life and in the lives of others.

When you use your words to remind you of your purpose in life, you will inevitably move in the direction of the success that you seek.

If you can't devise full affirmations, consider at least creating a bank of power words that you can use to target any negative words and thoughts that threaten your peace of mind.

Create words you love and that make you feel good and inspire you to do good. Write them down, put the paper where you can see it on your desk, and say them several times a day.

Examples of really positive, uplifting words are: Innovative, generous, spirited, good-hearted, abundant, grateful, dedicated, and focused.

2) Read one enlightening, positive book a month.

Your mind is a well and you do not want that well to run dry. Fill it up regularly by absorbing new ideas, introducing new books with positive messages, and finding new perspectives on the world.

According to Pew Research Center, 27 percent of adults don't read a single book a year, and the average number of books most adults read is four. If you develop the habit of always having a book on the go, you will be amazed at how many fascinating books you can fill up your mind with each year.

Sometimes, my only time to read is when I have to wait for somebody or something or during a brief break in my day, perhaps an hour on the weekend and a few minutes some evenings.

Make a commitment to read a blog post from a writer who inspires you at least once a day. You can listen to audio books if you have to spend long hours on the road or listen to podcasts as you are getting ready for work in the morning. There is always a way to find time to fill up your well of inspiration.

3) Keep a Journal of Good Thoughts.

A few years ago, I learned that one of my friends started to jot down great quotations, ideas and thoughts from the material she was reading. She invested in a lovely journal and started noting the idea or quotation, the place she found it, and the time she read it. Sometimes she added her own thoughts about how a particular thought impacted her life, and how she would use it to move closer to her goals in the future.

At this point, she has filled six thick journals of good thoughts. I thought this was a wonderful idea and started doing the same. Sometimes if I feel negative words are filling my head or my mind is clouded with worry, I pull out one of the journals and within a few minutes, my balance of positivity has been restored.

You could start an online diary of good thoughts if you wish and it will work as well. Personally, the act of physically writing out the quotation or thought works for me because it commits it better to my memory.

4) Give genuine compliments and accept compliments graciously.

Practice using your words to evoke positive emotions by finding something nice to say to people as you encounter them. It is a rare person whose day is not brightened by hearing an authentic compliment.

Sometimes when we start to find things to compliment people about, we start with noticing a simple article of clothing or work that they have done. As we get to know them better, we begin to understand the depth of their knowledge or their positive attitude or their infectious smile.

It's okay to mention those things.

Genuine compliments are not silly flatteries. They are an authentic way to send a message to another person that you appreciate them and respect their fine points.

When someone gives you a nice compliment, learn to accept it graciously and cherish it. Tuck it into your well for positive self-talk in the future.

5) Engage in positive self-talk.

When you doubt yourself, when your feelings get hurt or someone you care about fails to meet your expectations, it is easy to fall into negative self-talk.

As soon as you recognize it, it is important to turn it around and change it to positive self-talk. That is difficult for most of us, but not impossible.

One technique that has worked well with my clients is to build a habit of engaging in positive self-talk deliberately at the times of the day when we start to doubt ourselves. These are traditionally early in the morning, late at night, as tiredness hits in the late afternoon, and when we are over-worked or over-stressed.

Force yourself to stop the stream of negative thoughts pouring through your brain by clearing you brain with three long, deep breaths.

Then tell yourself how well you are doing, how your special skill is going to pull this challenge together for you, and how your great attitude is going to save the day. The more you tell yourself this, the more likely it will become a self-fulfilling prophecy.

Something to think about:

I am constantly seeking better, positive and up lifting words to say, that will enhance my life and the lives of others.

I believe that it is essential in life to challenge the words that limit us and paralyze us from living our potential.

Regardless of your perspective, developing an intentional attitude about your word use is of primary importance in tapping into your authentic power. How will you find your own unique ways to turn negative words into positive words for your future success?

Something to do:

I hope you can use some of the strategies discussed in this book to become more conscious of the impact of your thoughts and words, and develop new ones that work for you. Either way, it is vital that you become more conscious of what you allow to dominate your thoughts.

Your words have the power to transform you and your life. For this final exercise, visualize in words the success that you seek and refer to it often. Let it fill your heart and your thoughts and guide you to your success.

APPENDIX

Chapter One
How words can haunt you

Answer honestly: Were you verbally bullied as a child or adolescent? What words hurt the most? What negative words directed at you colored how you perceive yourself as an adult?

Make a list of three things that others told you about yourself that hurt and that keep circling in your mind. We will work through these in the upcoming chapters and help you to remove them from the thought-loop that goes through your head when you feel challenged and afraid that you will not be able to accomplish what you want to do.

Conversely, were you one of the lucky people who grew up with encouraging words? Which of those words gives up courage when you are faced with a major challenge? Which of those words do you share with others to connect with their confidence and reinforce it?

Chapter Two
You can create a new reality with words

Do you have continuing negative thoughts or phrases that roll through your head repeatedly? How do those thoughts make you feel when you stop and dwell on them?

If you suspect that words are leading you to darkness instead of life, start to consider a strategy for change. In the upcoming chapters you will receive lots of ideas and prompts, but start now to consider your position to change.

Chapter Three
How your complaints make your world smaller

If you are trying to break the habit of complaining, start a gratitude journal today. List or write about the things that you are thankful for and that bring joy to your life.

If your negativity stems by living with someone who constantly complains or hanging out with friends who gripe about the world at every opportunity, begin to set boundaries. You don't have to mindlessly agree with them but you can use up a lot of energy and time trying to change their minds and still fail. If they persist, do your best to limit the amount of time you spend with them.

Just as you would not invite a smoker into your home to pollute it and expose you to harmful carcinogens, you do not have to make a lot of time in your schedule for a chronic complainer who refuses to explore the positive parts of life.

At the end of the day, understand that as much as you would like everyone in your life to be happy, you cannot make that happen. We are all responsible for our own happiness and well-being.

Chapter Four
Unleash the power of positive words

Focus on the words that are most commonly used by you in conversation. A good way to do that is to look at an email, record a conversation or take notes while you are someone else talks. Are you sprinkling your daily chats with loads of positive words that people respond to favorably, or do you see the darker, negative side of things and describe your day, your work and your home life through a filter of negativity?

Tomorrow, make a conscious effort to get through the day using only positive words with happy connotations.

Chapter Five
How words and ideas can change our world

Think about one cause that matters to you passionately. Write just one short paragraph of words you would use to persuade someone else to care about it as well.

Chapter Six
How words guide our modern technology

Never underestimate the power of one small well-expressed sentiment. Think about the many websites that generate high traffic just by offering a collection of quotations.

Think about how these three quotes make you feel and try to pick up the keywords that trigger your emotional responses:

"The only person you are destined to become is the person you decide to be." – Ralph Waldo Emerson

"Happiness is when what you think, what you say, and what you do are in harmony" – Mahatma Gandhi

"Every great dream begins with a dreamer. Always remember, you have within you the strength, the patience, and the passion to reach for the stars to change the world." – Harriet Tubman

Chapter Seven
The case for leaving some words unsaid Something to do:

The power of words exists whether you want to use them for good or bad. Think about the last serious verbal disagreement you had with a colleague or loved one. What kind of tactics did you use to get your point of view across? Knowing what you know now, how would you change your verbal exchanges?

Chapter Eight
How words can change your brain for the better

Write three adjectives that best describe your career potential. Next, put them in context by giving an illustration example that illustrates why that adjective is an accurate way to describe yourself.

Chapter Nine
Words that may be used to manipulate you and others

If you spend time with a person who makes you feel uncomfortable and unfulfilled, listen to their words and try to determine if that feeling is coming from being manipulated.

What words or phrases are being used that cause your red flags to go up? How can you change this relationship by asserting yourself and refusing to be manipulated?

Chapter Ten
How you can use your words to grow your success

I hope you can use some of the strategies discussed in this book to become more conscious of the impact of your thoughts and words, and develop new ones that work for you. Either way, it is vital that you become more conscious of what you allow to dominate your thoughts.

Your words have the power to transform you and your life. For this final exercise, visualize in words the success that you seek and refer to it often. Let it fill your heart and your thoughts and guide you to your success.

CONCLUSION

People who pay attention to and let words lead them to success fully understand the power of words. They know that even the words we allow to dominate our minds internally will guide us and ultimately, they will pour out of us and guide others.

These words build our destiny. Successful people know they must control their words and thoughts, rather than let their words and thoughts control them. They use positive affirmations, respect, encouragement and love in their words to guild their actions.

If you want success, your words need to be aligned with your goals. Your visions and your dreams all need to be on the same page and in the same tone as the words that you speak.

As much as your words can do, they can be even more powerful and purposeful when you use them to help other people achieve positivity in their own lives.

You have the power to uplift others as well as yourself, and that is a special privilege your words grant you. With simple phrases and a mere 26-letter alphabet, you can find a way to make people believe in themselves, feel respected and safe, and be inspired to be their best.

Words are powerful in guiding your own destiny it is true. But they are more powerful still in helping others towards positive change.

BIBLIOGRAPHY

Bowen, Will. *A Complaint Free World: How to stop complaining and start enjoying the life you always wanted.* Harmony Publishing. Feb. 5, 2013

Branden, Nathaniel. *The Six Pillars of Self-Esteem: The Definitive Work on Self-esteem by the Leading Pioneer in the Field.* Bantam Publishing. May 1, 1995

Carmody, Dennis P. and Lewis, Michael. Brain activation when hearing one's own and other's names. *Brain Res.* Oct. 20, 2006. P. 153-158

Cromie, William J. Verbal beatings hurt as much as sexual abuse: can lead to depression, anxiety and worse. *The Harvard Gazette.* April 26, 2007

Dan Rockwell, Inc. Magazine Top 50 Leadership Expert. "Leadership is positive influence, not malicious manipulation."

Frederickson, BL. Updated Thinking on Positivity Ratios. *American Psychologist.* Advance online publication. Doi 10.10 37/ a0033584. July 15, 2013

Hampel, H. et al. Core candidate neurochemical and imaging biomarkers of Alzheimer's disease. US Library of Medicine, National Institute of Health. Dec. 21, 2007

Katie, Byron and Mitchell, Stephen. *Loving What Is: Four Questions That Can Change Your Life.* Three Rivers Press. Dec. 23, 2003

Knowledge.Wharton.openn.edu. How what you say reveals more than you think. Feb. 16, 2018

Lyubomirsky, Sonya. *The How of Happiness: A Scientific Approach to Getting the Life You Want.* Penguin. Dec. 27, 2007

Mehl, Matthias R. et al. Narcissism and the Use of Personal Pronouns Revisited. *Journal of Personality and Social Psychology.* 2015, Vol. 109, No. 3, e1-e15.

Newberg, Andrew B. and Waldman, Mark Robert. *Words Can Change Your Brain: 12 Conversation Strategies to Build Trust, Resolve Conflict, and Increase Intimacy.* Penguin Group (USA) June 14, 2012

Pennebaker, Dr. James. *The Secret Life of Pronouns: What our words say about us.* Bloomsbury Press. Jan. 15, 2013

Phillips, Dr. Betty. "Imagine a Complaint Free World." Advice Line. ChathamCountyLine.org. February, 2009

Schwartz, Mark. "Robert Sapolsky discussed physiological effects of stress." Stanford University News. March 7, 2007

Talavage, TM, Gonzalez-Castillo J., and Scott, Sophie. Auditory neuroimaging with fMRI and PET. *Hearing Research.* 307 4-15, 2014.

The University of Vermont News Service (www.uvm.edu). F-bombs notwithstanding, all languages skew toward happiness. (About research of Chris Danforth and Peter Dodds). Feb. 9, 2015

Thibodeau, P.H. and Boroditsky, L. Metaphors We Think With: The Role of Metaphor in Reasoning. *Plos ONE.* 2011. 6,e16782.

Wagner, Daniel. *White Bears and Other Unwanted Thoughts: Suppression, Obsession, and the Psychology of Mental Control.* The Guilford Press. May 1, 1984

Wang, Ming-Te and Kenny, Sarah. Longitudinal links between fathers' and mothers' harsh verbal discipline and adolescents' conduct problems and depressive symptoms. *Child Development.* Vol. 95, Issue 3, Pages 908-923. Sept. 3, 2013

Winch, Dr. Guy. *The Squeaky Wheel: Complaining the Right Way to Get Results, Improve Your Relationships and Enhance Self-Esteem.* Walker and Company Publishers. Jan. 31, 2011

ABOUT THE AUTHOR

This is the third book authored by JoAnn Youngblood King, Certified Success Coach (CTA), owner of Live Your Potential, a coaching company that has assisted many people achieve personal success in their lives.

It continues to grow her mandate to help as many people as possible lead full and successful lives and reaching their full potential.

Her coaching style has been described by her clients as "relaxed and effective."

Her coaching is delivered by phone and email.

"JoAnn is such a positive person and is able to bring out the best in everyone who interacts with her," says a recent client. "She helped steer me down a path I wanted to take but was having trouble finding the courage to pursue. She has made a difference in helping me achieve success beyond what I could have imagined."

Her motto is: "You have the potential inside for great success. Now is the time to Live Your Potential."

This book emerged from her belief that the words we think and say often dictate the paths we take in life. Words shape us and our destiny.

JoAnn has been coaching professionally since 2004.

www.ingramcontent.com/pod-product-compliance
Lightning Source LLC
Chambersburg PA
CBHW071839290426
44109CB00017B/1866